DATE DUE		
AUG. 5 1982		
JAN. 1 3 1983		
FEB. 7 1983		
FEB. 2 3 1983		
MAR, 1 2 1983		
SEP. 1 2 1984		
SEP. 2 7 1984		
FE 1 9 85		
MR 5 '87		
MY 2 0 '87		
JE 1 6 '92		
AP 1 0 '02		
MY 0 6 09		
201-6503		Printed in USA

MICHIGAN
A PICTURE BOOK TO REMEMBER HER BY

Designed and Produced by
TED SMART and DAVID GIBBON

CRESCENT BOOKS
NEW YORK

INTRODUCTION

"...a flowering solitude, delightful and scented; a magnificent dwelling, a living palace built for man" was the unforgettable impression made on an adventurous French politician and lawyer, Alexis de Tocqueville when he took a boat trip down the Saginaw river in 1831. Aptly named by its early Indian inhabitants, Michigan, meaning "big water", despite enormous changes over the past one hundred and fifty years can still evoke those feelings in its visitors. Modern day Michigan displays a sharply contrasted landscape of successful industrial cities punctuating vast expanses of wooded wilderness and modern state highways contradicting narrow dirt tracks that weave in and out of the small rustic villages. This dichotomy, in some ways, echoes the years of strife that have coloured Michigan's history; however, its flourishing present day industries quickly dispel any suspicions that the wounds incurred by the bitter wars over leadership never healed.

French explorers, in search of a passage to the Orient in the early seventeenth century, first mapped this unknown territory north of Ohio and east of the Mississippi. Finding a land not only surrounded by water on all sides, except the south, by four of the great lakes, but also with more than eleven thousand smaller lakes, rivers and streams, they soon realised the potential of an area abundant in trees and fur-bearing animals. With the help of two of the Indian tribes already resident there, the Ottowa and Chippewa, the French developed a lucrative fur-trapping business, and in 1701 a French soldier and explorer, Antoine de La Mothe Cadillac, established Detroit, now the most important city in the state, as a fur trading post.

Michigan remained allied to Canada until 1783 when it was designated a part of the United States, although in 1760 the English defeated the French and at the signing of the Treaty of Paris took leadership over Canada and the majority of the French colonial land east of the Mississippi. The year 1805 saw the separation of Michigan from Indiana territory and from then on it flourished as an American polity and was admitted to the union in 1837 as the 26th state.

Then began a rapid internal improvement plan, building roads, canals and developing cities to promote its quickly-growing industries. The land, dramatically cut into two peninsulas, accommodates most of its inhabitants in the lower peninsula but, bursting with colourful woodland and luscious, gently rolling hills, the more sparsely populated upper peninsula is by no means a barren waste. Rivers teeming with fish are a sportsman's paradise and the timberland, carefully restored after the rapacious felling of the early settlers, is now the leafy home of numerous deer and bears.

Contributing less to income in the state than either agriculture or manufacturing, mining, particularly of iron ore, places Michigan as an important mineral producing state. Popular hearsay suggests that the upper peninsula could provide enough salt to supply the whole world for the next million years.

Less wild, but no less beautiful, the lower peninsula is a very different sort of country. Many of the southern counties have acres of golden maize and corn fields, another lucrative industry; and the shores of Lake Michigan are lined with the state's renowned fruit belt. Although no longer the capital, the importance of Detroit cannot be overstressed. Its massive automobile industry, the core of the early twentieth century industrial revolution, feeds the nearby cities of Flint, the state capital Lansing, Saginaw, Ypsilanti and Kalamazoo, and is the largest in the United States.

Perhaps, then, it is too much to expect that Michigan, so successful in industry, also attracts visitors. Certainly it lacks the New Yorkian vitality and cannot boast the awesomeness of the Grand Canyon, but Michigan's scenery, with hills carpeted in snow in the winter, magnificent lakeside views and an exciting history restored in buildings, churches and museums, captures the hearts of many American and overseas visitors.

The "Spirit of Detroit" *left,* symbolises the verve behind the city's rebirth, which is immortalized in the glittering Detroit skyline *overleaf,* the epitome of modern America.

Behind 20th-century Detroit's diverse
architectural designs, lies a single aim – the
successful future of the city's massive
redevelopment plan, an aim to which
Dodge Fountain in Hart Plaza *above*, the
Medical Centre *right* and Fisher Building
below, have all remained faithful. The
brightly coloured tram *left* glides along
Washington Boulevard to the recreational
area of Cobo Hall. Silhouetted against the
evening sky, the graceful Ambassador
Bridge *overleaf* spans the Detroit River.

Soaring skyscrapers in downtown Detroit dwarf the river's bank *above* and surround the Hart Plaza *top left,* and the Detroit Science Centre *bottom left* prides itself on its unique exhibition style. The magnificent Renaissance Centre *right,* with its futuristic interior *overleaf,* is a memorable mark of the city's progression, while the "Shrine of the Little Flower" church *below* and ornate James Scott Fountain *centre left,* which dominates Belle Isle Park, retain all the charm of Detroit's colourful past.

The world-famous Henry Ford museum in Dearborn boasts a wealth of restored vintage vehicles *these pages,* and is one of the many fine exhibits portraying the city's industrial growth spanning the past three centuries. Adjacent to the museum, Greenfield Village *overleaf,* is a 240 acre complex of some 85 historic structures which reproduce early life in America.

Henry Ford Museum

A carriage ride down quiet lanes *top right,* past authentic reproductions of homes and stores *centre and bottom right and below,* displays Greenfield Village as a fulfilment of Henry Ford's promise "When we are through we shall have reproduced American life as lived…" Independence Hall, symbol of American Liberty *left,* stands at the entrance to his museum of history, which Ford dedicated, together with the village, to Thomas Edison. Nearby is sited the Ford Motor Company's world headquarters *above,* known as "The Glass House".

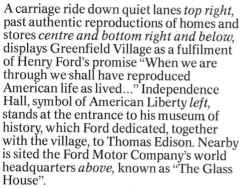

The Blue Water Bridge *left*, completed in 1938, crosses the three and a half mile distance over the St Clair River between Port Huron and Sarnia in Canada, and the industrial town of Flint *above* was the birthplace of General Motors. Indicative of the state's steady climb to success is the famous historical figure of Thomas Edison, the technological genius and pioneer of motion-pictures who, as the plaque *below* explains, spent his early years in Detroit.

Ann Arbor is most famous for the University of Michigan, and Burton Memorial Tower *right* contains the Baird Carillon consisting of fifty five bells.

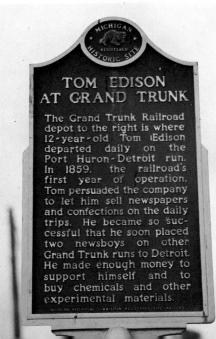

MICHIGAN REGISTERED HISTORIC SITE

TOM EDISON AT GRAND TRUNK

The Grand Trunk Railroad depot to the right is where 12-year-old Tom Edison departed daily on the Port Huron-Detroit run. In 1859, the railroad's first year of operation, Tom persuaded the company to let him sell newspapers and confections on the daily trips. He became so successful that he soon placed two newsboys on other Grand Trunk runs to Detroit. He made enough money to support himself and to buy chemicals and other experimental materials.

MICHIGAN HISTORICAL COMMISSION REGISTERED SITE NO. 203

East Michigan affords a wealth of scenic countryside and the town of Frankenmuth, settled by Germans whose story is recounted *below,* colourfully displays its Bavarian heritage in the charming Inn *above* and by the Christmas decorations inside 'Bronners' store *left.*

Dow Gardens *right* are the original gardens of Dr Dow, and in keeping with his love for nature in realistic settings, the grounds are emblazoned with colourful flowers and trees all the year round.

The picturesque lighthouse *above right,* stands watch over Lake Michigan at the tip of the Leelanau Peninsula.

MICHIGAN'S GERMAN SETTLERS

Fifteen German immigrants from Franconia, Bavaria, led by the Rev. August Craemer, founded Frankenmuth in 1845. They were advised to settle here by the Rev. Frederick Schmid, Lutheran pastor of Ann Arbor's German colony, founded in the 1820's. Other German agricultural villages were founded in the Saginaw Valley in the 1840's and '50's. Here, as in many other areas of Michigan, German settlers have contributed greatly to the state's cultural heritage.

Throughout the 19th century, Michigan played host to a variety of cultures which are evident throughout the state in its landscape and architectural designs. Holland, at the mouth of the Black River, was settled in 1846 and Windmill Island *above* provides the perfect environment for "De Zwaan" *right*, set in leafy surroundings every bit as charming as its original home. In majestic contrast, the State Capitol *left* rises in the heart of Lansing, surmounted by a dome similar to that of the White House in Washington D.C. The War Memorial *below* is sited at Grand Rapids, Michigan's second largest city.

The Lincoln Memorial *right* is attractively situated in the spacious port city of Muskegon, with its more contemporary city hall *left*. Formerly known as the "Lumber Queen of the World", the days when the city thrived with the logging industry are remembered in the name of the river bank *below*.

Rising luxuriously from glittering water, the folding sand dunes *above* add to the beauty of Silver Lake State Park near Muskegon.

LUMBERMAN'S BANK

Towards the tip of the Upper Peninsula, Houghton is the gateway to a popular resort area, graced with some two hundred thousand acres of state forests, and Houghton Lake *above, below and top and bottom right* is the largest inland lake in Michigan.

The farm in Wexford *centre right* is a modern contrast to the Historical Museum in its neighbouring county of Manistee, where a fully reconstructed Victorian store *left and overleaf* is one of the many fine exhibits.

The scenic Sleeping Bear Dunes *bottom and centre left and right* near Frankfort *top left,* is one of the largest shifting dunes in the world, rising 480 feet above Lake Michigan. Point Betsie Lighthouse *above* sits on a beautiful sandy point five miles north of Frankfort, and a picturesque drive extending the length of Old Mission Peninsula passes Leaning Barn *below* and leads to Old Mission Lighthouse *overleaf,* one of the first lighthouses to be built overlooking the Great Lakes, sited at the tip of the peninsula.

The placid waters of Lake Michigan surrounding the delightful district of Leland in the Leelanau Peninsula *below, right and above and below left,* contain some of the best fresh-water trout, salmon and white-fish in the state. Nearby, the splendid old school house, converted into an antique shop *above,* emerges from the dense woodland that lines the quiet roads.

Overleaf: Evening gradually descends over the softly rippling surface of Traverse Bay in Lake Michigan.

LELAND HISTORIC DISTRICT (FISHTOWN)

This commercial fishing district has provided a livelihood for residents of the town for over a century. Fishermen reached the fishing grounds of Lake Michigan by way of the Leland River (Carp River) using small sailboats until the introduction of primitive gas powered oak boats around 1900. Small fishing shanties and related buildings such as ice and smoke houses were constructed during the peak years of the industry which spanned the first three decades of the twentieth century. Now gray and weather-beaten, some still serve their original purpose. Other buildings in the district date back to Leland's lumbering and logging era in the latter half of the nineteenth century. Leland continues to be a commercial fishing center and will also serve as the headquarters for transport to the Manitou Islands.

Vineyards are a prominent feature of West Michigan's countryside and Travers City is no exception with the Chateau Grand Travers *above* and vineyards *left*. Throughout the year, festivals take place where vineyard tours, wine-tasting and grape stomping are among the most popular events.

Michigan's only wild-life ranch, Game Haven, overlooks the beautiful Sturgeon River Valley in Wolverine. An exciting variety of animals roam freely in undisturbed surroundings and the popular Trophy House *opposite page* displays over 150 different species of wildlife.

Called Michilimackinac (Great Turtle) by the Indians, time and usage have shortened the name of the quaint island centering Lake Huron to Mackinac, and viewed *overleaf* from its Fort. This limestone outcrop became a frontier post in 1788 when the old French Garrison was moved from the mainland to its more strategic position on the island, and for some 115 years it remained the stronghold of the Straits of Mackinac. Only three miles long and two miles wide, high cliffs mark the shoreline and caves, obscure rock formations and natural bridges make up the landscape.

SILVER TIP
GRIZZLY
BEAR

MULE DE

LYNX CAT

WATER BUFFALO

AFRICAN
BUSH
PIG

Furnished with lush greenery, Mackinac *below right*, includes Arch Rock *centre left*, Huron Street *bottom left* and The Grand Hotel *above and below* among its varied attractions. The largest crucifix in the world *top left* is sited at Indian River Catholic Shrine. The graceful Mackinac Bridge *overleaf* connects Michigan's Upper and Lower peninsulas.

GRAND HOTEL

Opened on July 10, 1887, the Grand Hotel was built by the Grand Rapids & Indiana and the Michigan Central railroads and the Detroit & Cleveland Navigation Company through the efforts of Sen. Francis B. Stockbridge. It is built of Michigan white pine. With its magnificent colonial porch, longest in the world, it is a classic example of gracious living seldom seen today. One of the outstanding landmarks on the Great Lakes, it is the world's largest summer hotel.

Fort Michilimackinac *above, below and centre right*, at the south end of Mackinac Bridge *top and bottom right*, is an authentic restoration of the French and British fort, constructed on the original foundations, and includes the stockade, King's storehouse, soldiers' barracks and a church. Mackinac Maritime Museum *left*, built in 1892, contains a variety of exhibits that recreate the story of transport on the Great Lakes.

FORT MICHILIMACKINAC

This fort, built about 1715, put French soldiers at the Straits for the first time since 1701. French authority ceased in 1761 when British troops entered the fort. On June 2, 1763, during Pontiac's uprising, Chippewa Indians seized the fort, killing most of the small force, and held it a year. When the British moved to Mackinac Island in 1781 this old fort soon reverted to the wilderness.

Sault Ste Marie *below left*, Michigan's oldest city, is the home of the great engineering marvel Soo Locks *centre and bottom right*, through which more than a hundred million tons of freight passes each shipping season. A ten mile narrated boat trip *top right and below* provides an excellent insight into how the vessels are moved from Lake Superior to Lake Huron. Lower Taquamenon Falls *overleaf* consists of a series of bubbling, frothy rapids.

Pictured Rocks, immortalized in Longfellow's poem 'Hiawatha' were designated a national lakeshore in 1966. This magnificent area stretches 40 miles along Lake Superior, between Grand Marais and Munising, where sand dunes, colourful sandstone formations topped with forests and delicate waterfalls *left*, are among the many beautiful sights. Miners Castle *above*, so named for its mediaeval turrets, rises some 100 feet above Lake Superior. Taquamenon Falls *below and right*, are located in a 19,000 acre state park, 70 miles north of Mackinac. The Upper Falls, some 200 feet wide, plunge more than 40 feet to meet the water below, while within walking distance, the Lower Falls are a staircase of cascades edged by dense forests.

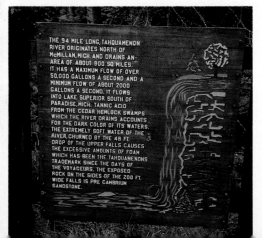

THE 94 MILE LONG, TAHQUAMENON RIVER ORIGINATES NORTH OF McMILLAN, MICH. AND DRAINS AN AREA OF ABOUT 900 SQ. MILES. IT HAS A MAXIMUM FLOW OF OVER 50,000 GALLONS A SECOND AND A MINIMUM FLOW OF ABOUT 2000 GALLONS A SECOND. IT FLOWS INTO LAKE SUPERIOR SOUTH OF PARADISE, MICH. TANNIC ACID FROM THE CEDAR HEMLOCK SWAMPS WHICH THE RIVER DRAINS ACCOUNTS FOR THE DARK COLOR OF ITS WATERS. THE EXTREMELY SOFT WATER OF THE RIVER, CHURNED BY THE 48 FT. DROP OF THE UPPER FALLS CAUSES THE EXCESSIVE AMOUNTS OF FOAM WHICH HAS BEEN THE TAHQUAMENONS TRADEMARK SINCE THE DAYS OF THE VOYAGEURS. THE EXPOSED ROCK ON THE SIDES OF THE 200 FT. WIDE FALLS IS PRE CAMBRIUM SANDSTONE.

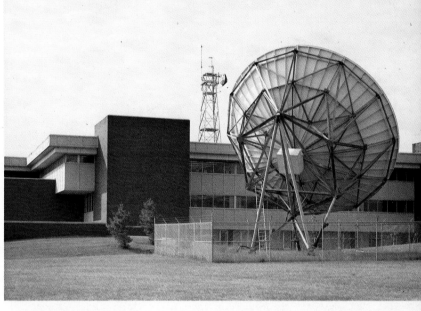

The beauty of Michigan's Upper Peninsula is nowhere more evident than Presque Isle Point *above* and *below left*, overlooking Lake Superior. The principal city, Marquette *top right*, is the home of Northern Michigan University *centre right*, and Paulson House *bottom right* described in the plaque *below*, is located in the nearby coastal town of Au Train.

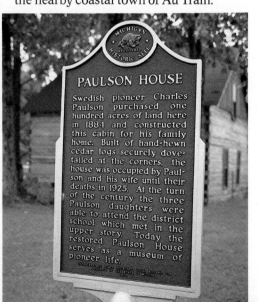

PAULSON HOUSE

Swedish pioneer Charles Paulson purchased one hundred acres of land here in 1884 and constructed this cabin for his family home. Built of hand-hewn cedar logs securely dovetailed at the corners, the house was occupied by Paulson and his wife until their deaths in 1925. At the turn of the century the three Paulson daughters were able to attend the district school which met in the upper story. Today the restored Paulson House serves as a museum of pioneer life.

Tumbling down their rocky slopes, Canyon Falls near Alberta *below* and the cascades at Iron Mountain *right*, enhance the rustic Upper Peninsula countryside, where the Shrine of the Snowshoe Priest, Bishop Frederick Baraga *above*, overlooks Keweenaw Bay.

The 'ghost town' of Fayette once thrived with the iron smelting industry, when the Jackson Iron Company opened furnaces there in the latter half of the 19th century. When these closed, the town was virtually abandoned and today the opera house *top left* is part of the restored town *centre and bottom left* in Fayette State Park.

In 1844, Fort Wilkins was built as protection for copper miners and speculators against possible Indian attacks. Today, its buildings have been carefully restored *previous page and centre left* and form part of the Fort Wilkins State Park in the scenic resort area of Copper Harbour.

The harbour itself *right*, at the tip of the Keweenaw Peninsula, and Eagle Harbour Lighthouse *above*, are typical of the area's greatest attraction, its breathtaking natural beauty.

The towns of Houghton and Hancock, where the first great mineral strike in the western hemisphere took place, face each other across the narrowest part of Portage Lake and are connected by a lift bridge *bottom left*. In memory of a by-gone age, when lumps of pure copper could be found scattered along the shore, attracting miners from far and wide, the old copper mine *top left* stands on the bank of the deep blue lake.

The graciously decorated auditorium *overleaf* is that of the Calumet Theatre, built at the turn of this century, to provide entertainment for the local mining communities.

First published in 1981 by Colour Library International Ltd.
Illustrations and text ©: Colour Library International Ltd, 163 East 64th Street, New York 10021.
Colour separations by FERCROM, Barcelona, Spain.
Display and text filmsetting by Focus Photoset, London, England.
Printed by Cayfosa and bound by Eurobinder - Barcelona (Spain)
Published by Crescent Books, a division of Crown Publishers Inc.
Library of Congress Catalogue Card No. 81 65050
CRESCENT 1981

Dep. Leg. B. 24.897/81